SLOTHS DOING HUMAN THINGS

COLORING BOOK

BY BRANDON BISHOP
& JEANNIE KOTYNSKI

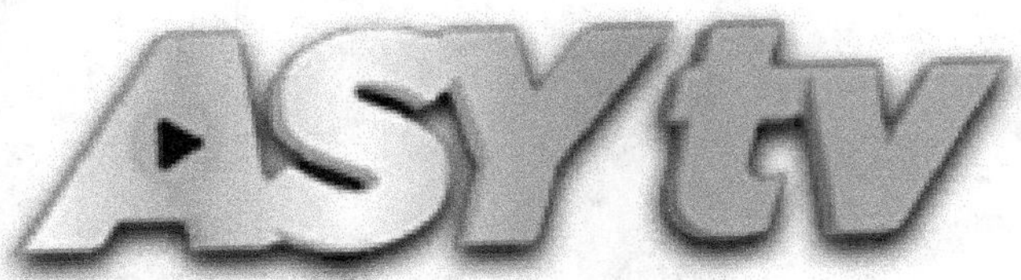

Sloths Doing Human Things Coloring Book

Written and Illustrated by Brandon Bishop & Jeannie Kotynski

Published by Burning Bulb Publishing, P.O. Box 4721, Bridgeport, WV 26330
ISBN: 978-1-948278-79-9

SLOTHS DOING HUMAN THINGS

The Coloring Book by Brandon Bishop & Jeannie Kotynski

Everything is all about parallel universes and infinite dimensions these days.

Well, if that's the case, then I am 100% certain that there's a timeline somewhere within the cosmos where sloths, yes, SLOTHS are the most dominant species on the planet, and they dress like and act as we humans do in our current dimension… albeit, slower than most humans… like REALLY slow… But effective nonetheless.

So in case you've ever wanted to see what sloths would look like doing human things, get your crayons and markers out, and let's bring this sloth universe to life!

I wonder what other animals we can dress up and put to work…

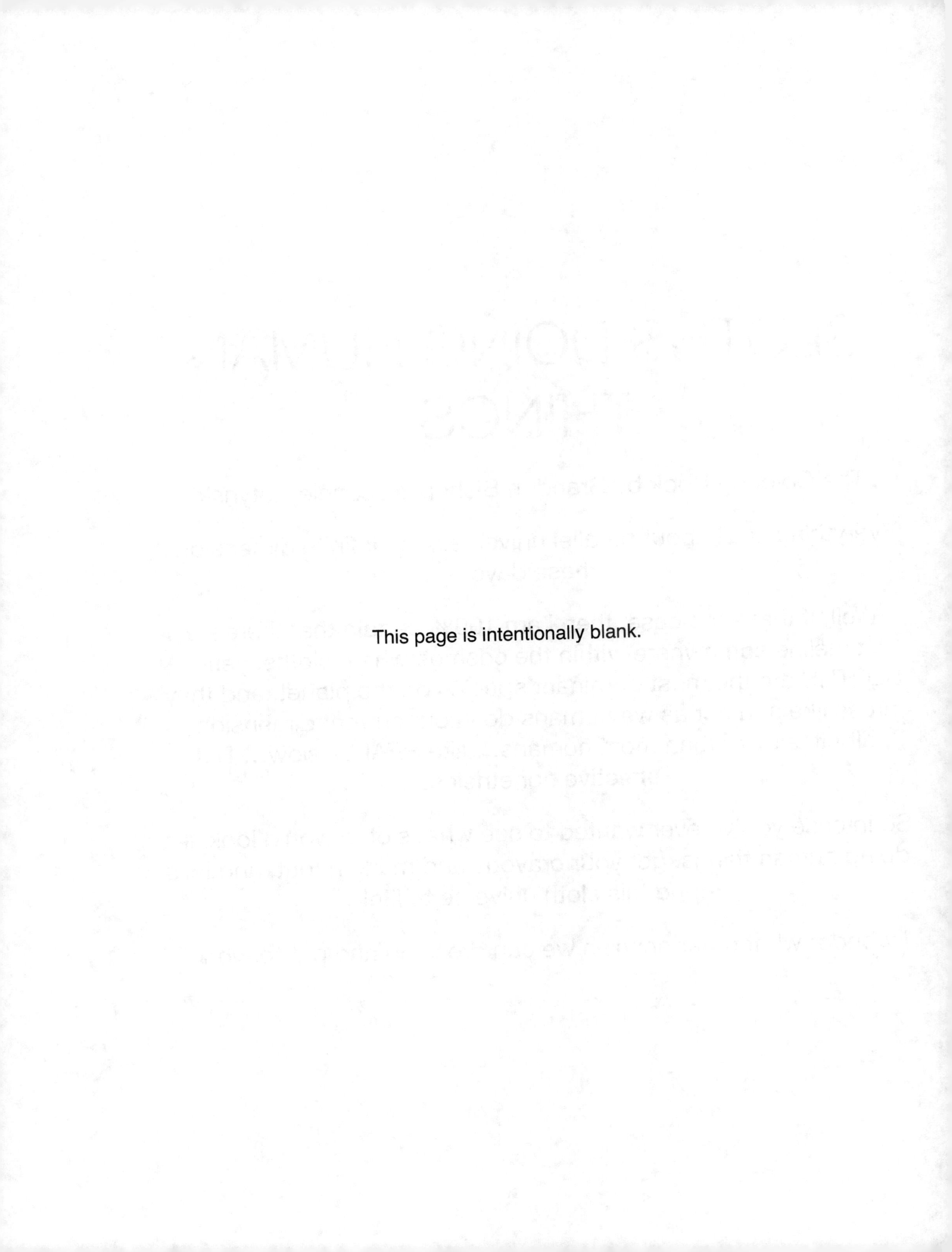

This page is intentionally blank.

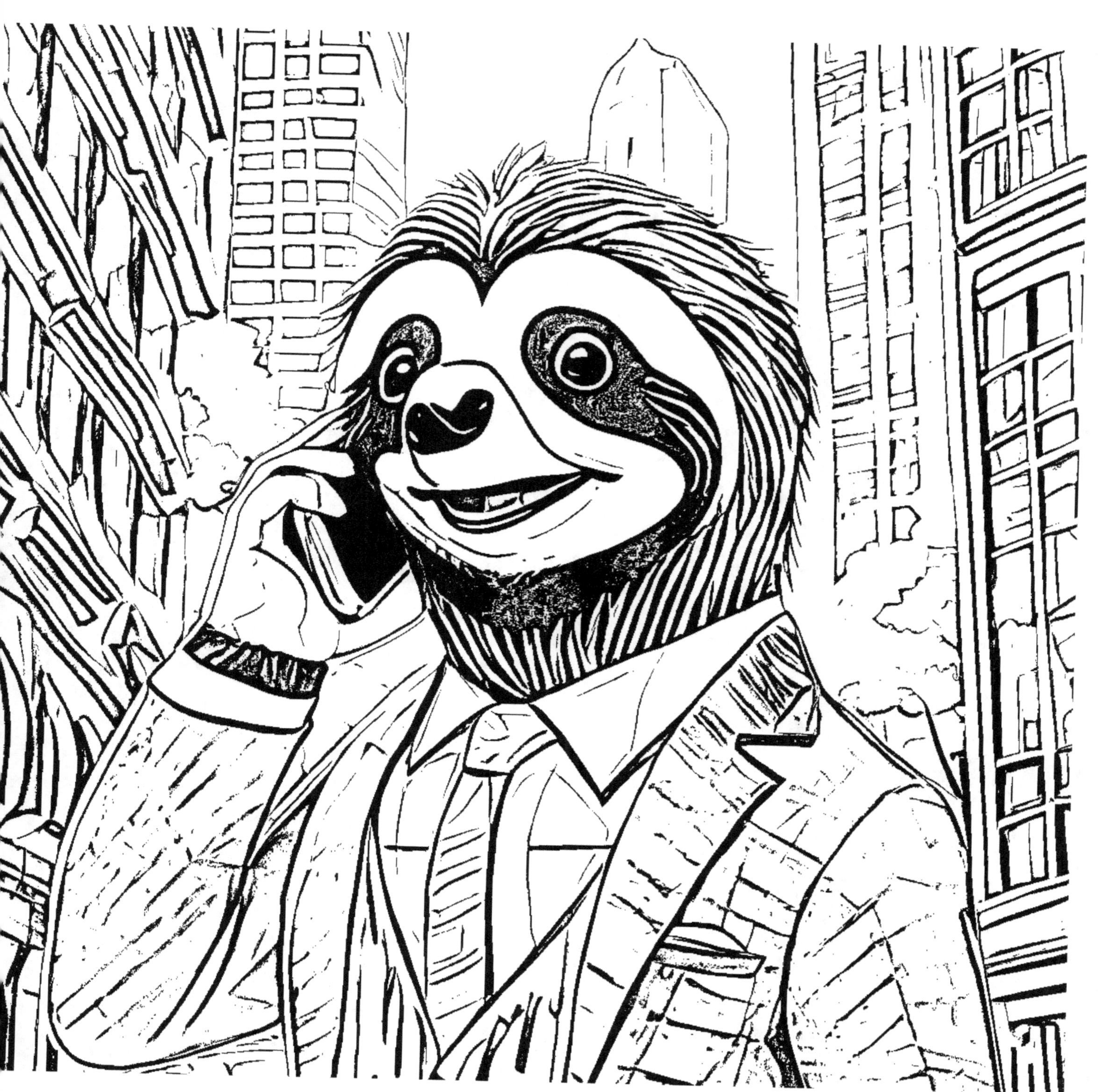

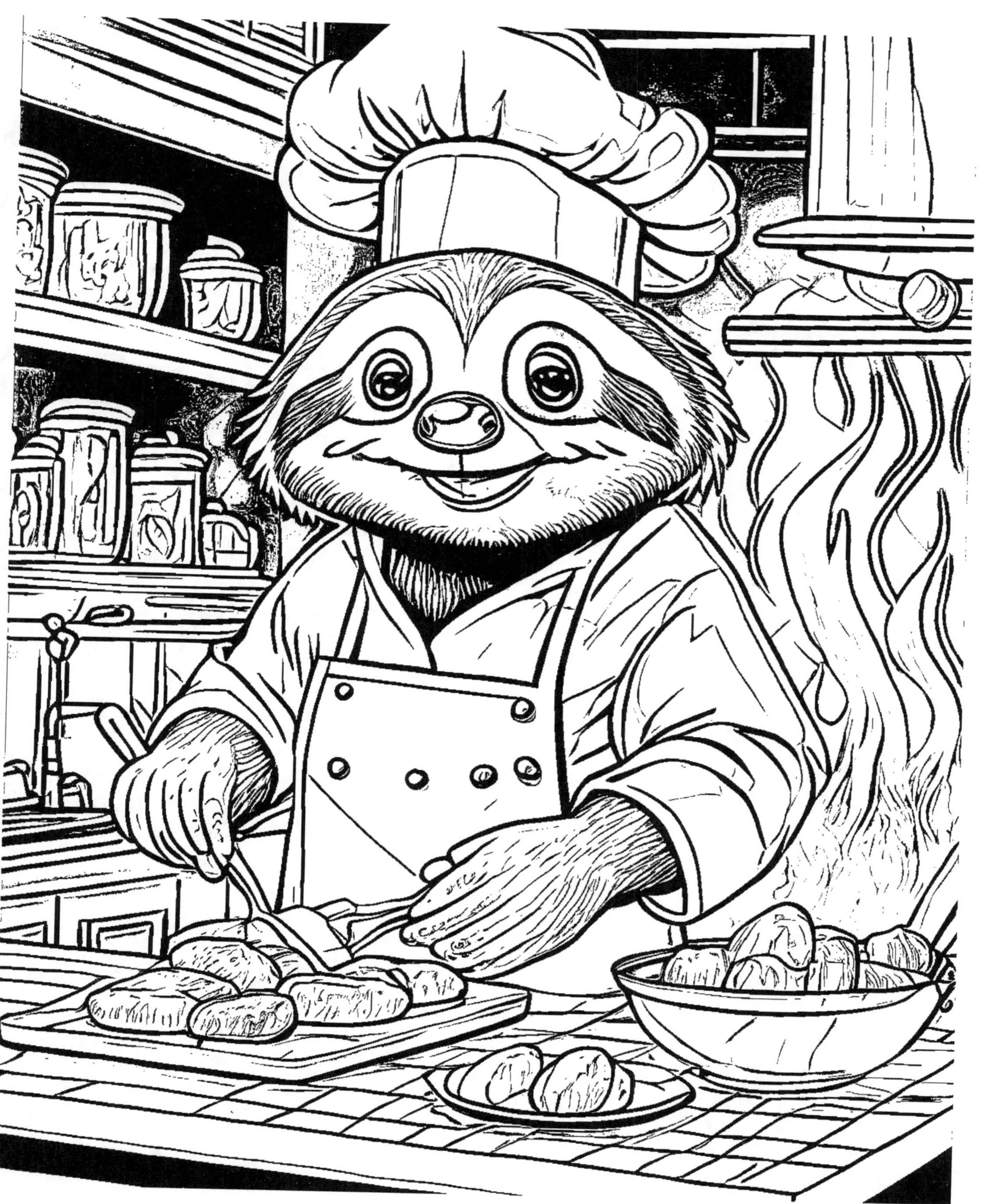

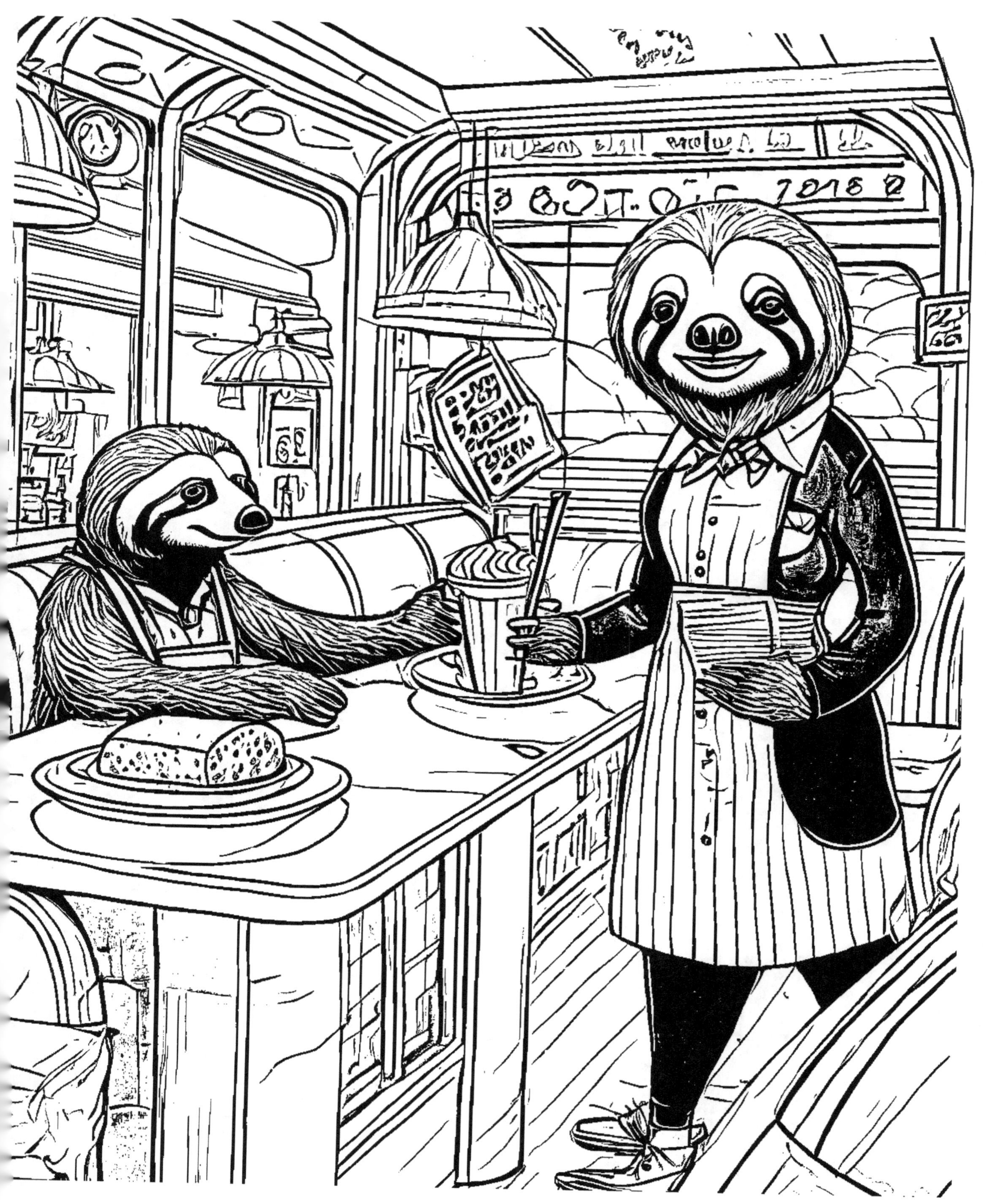

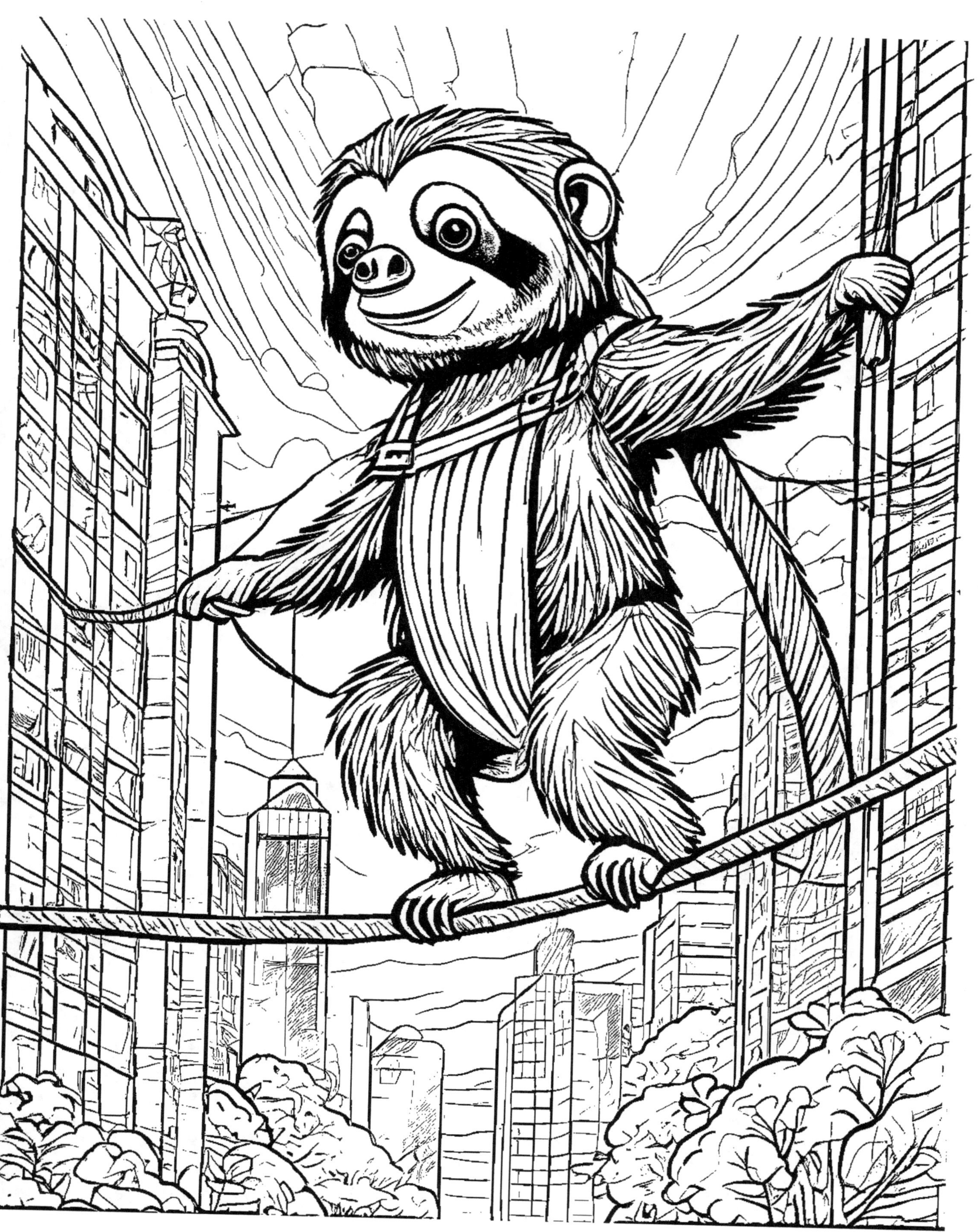

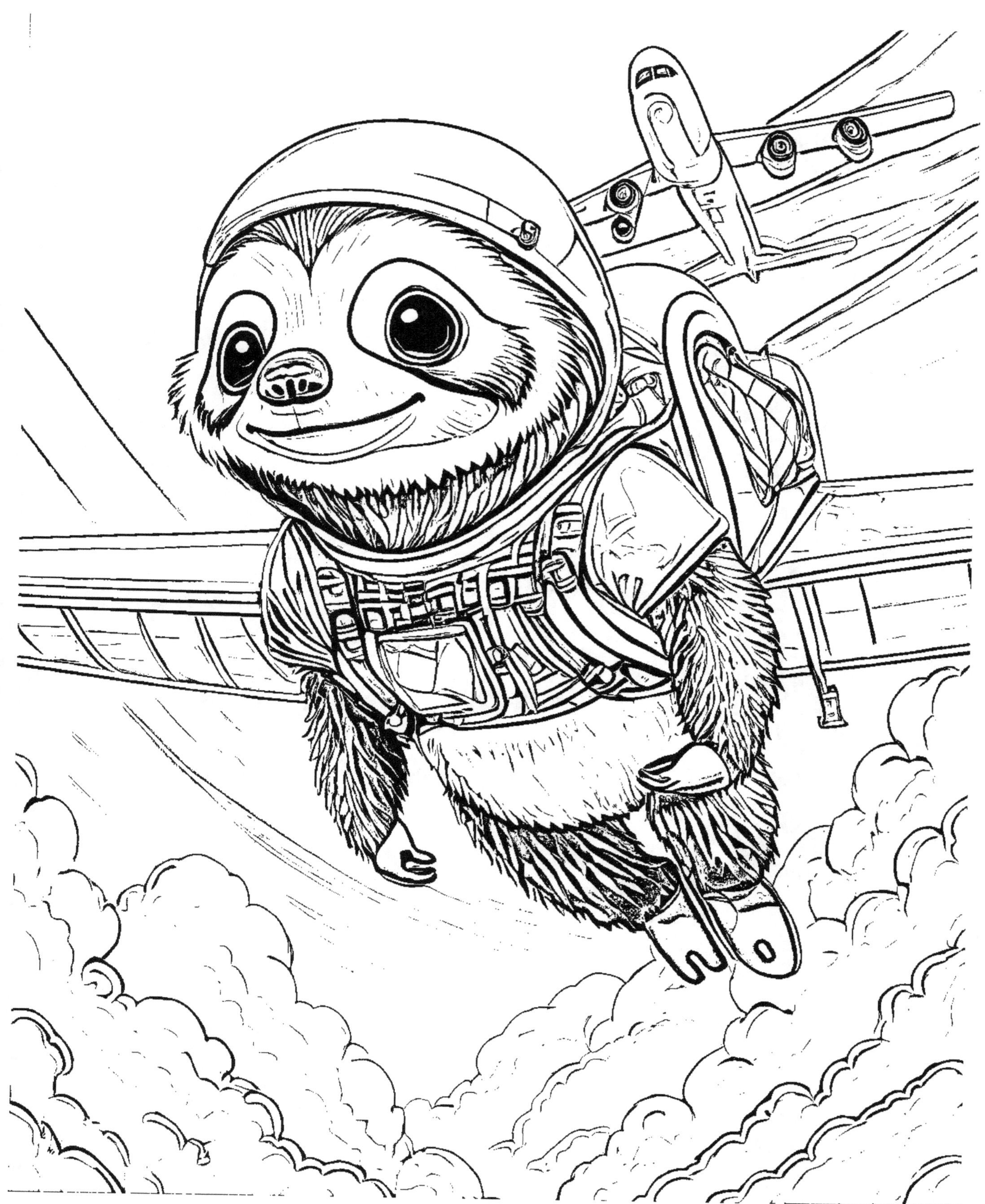

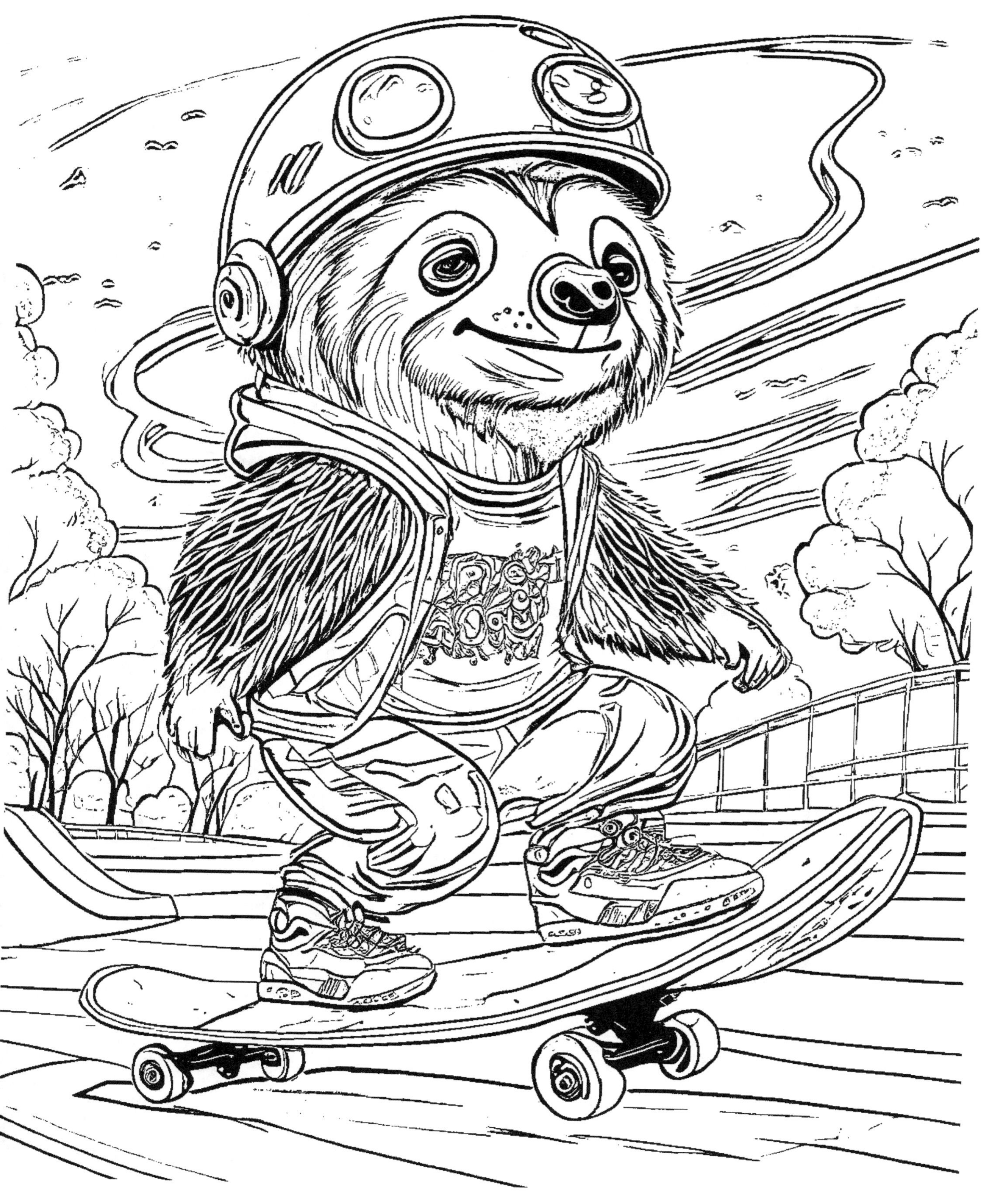

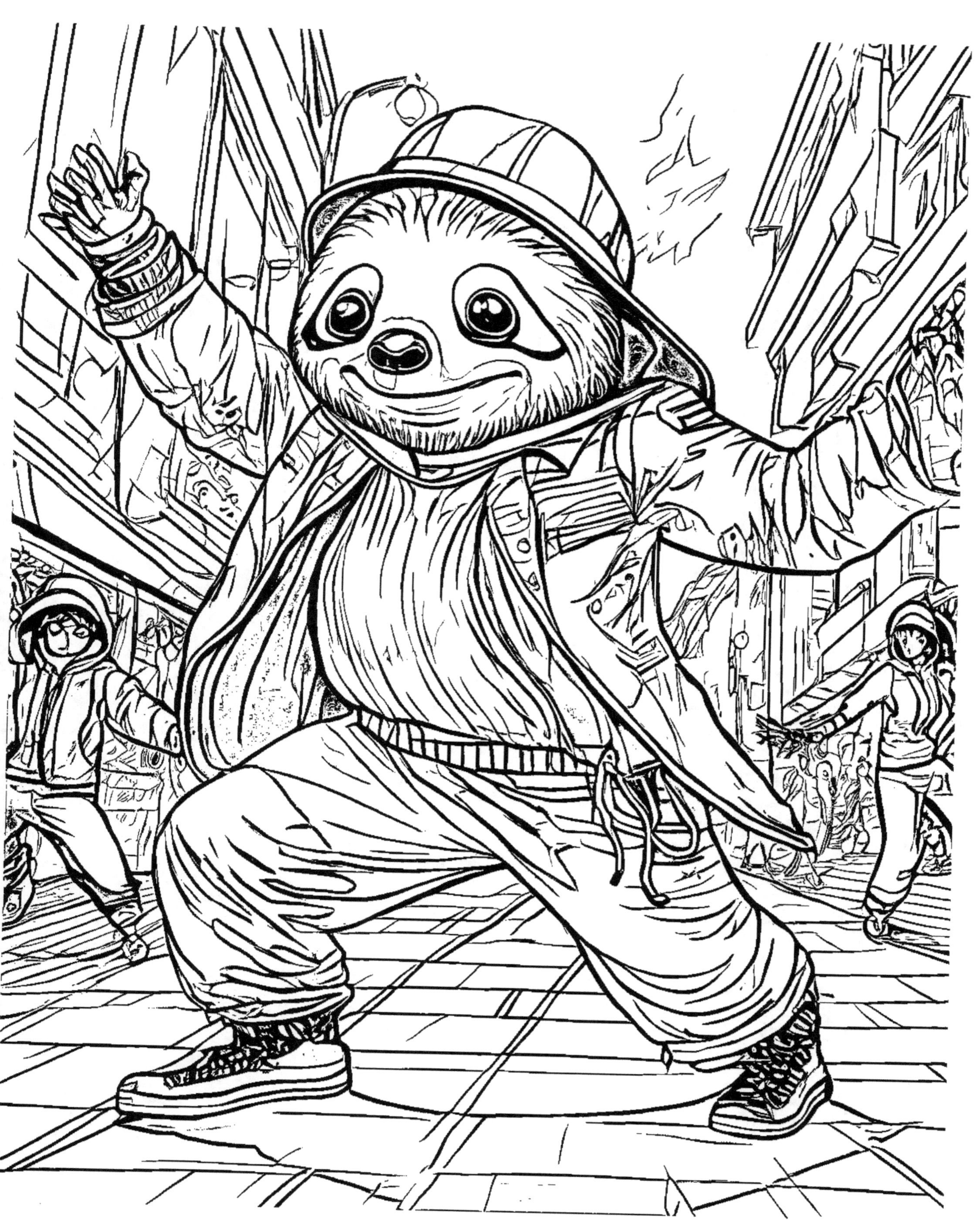

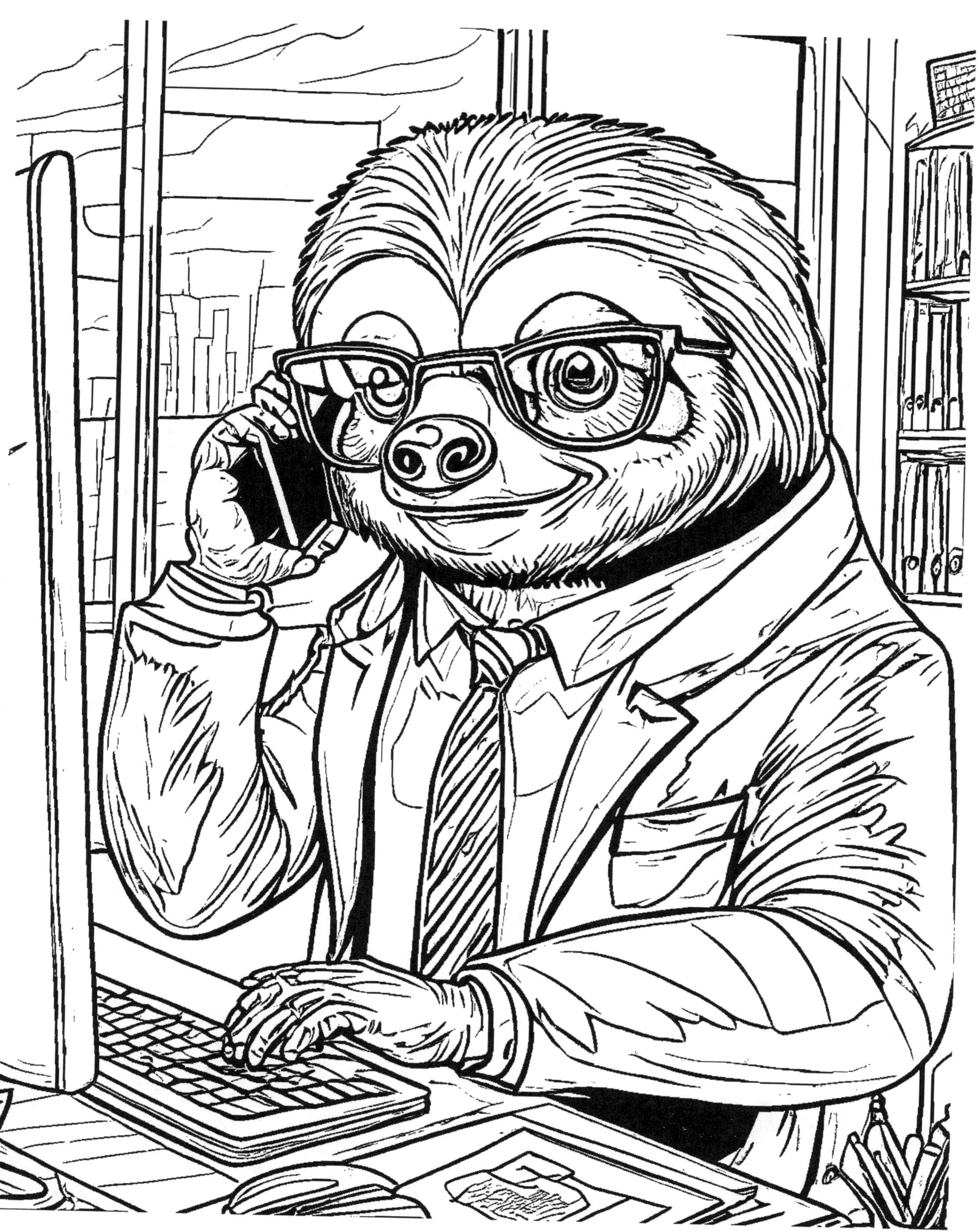

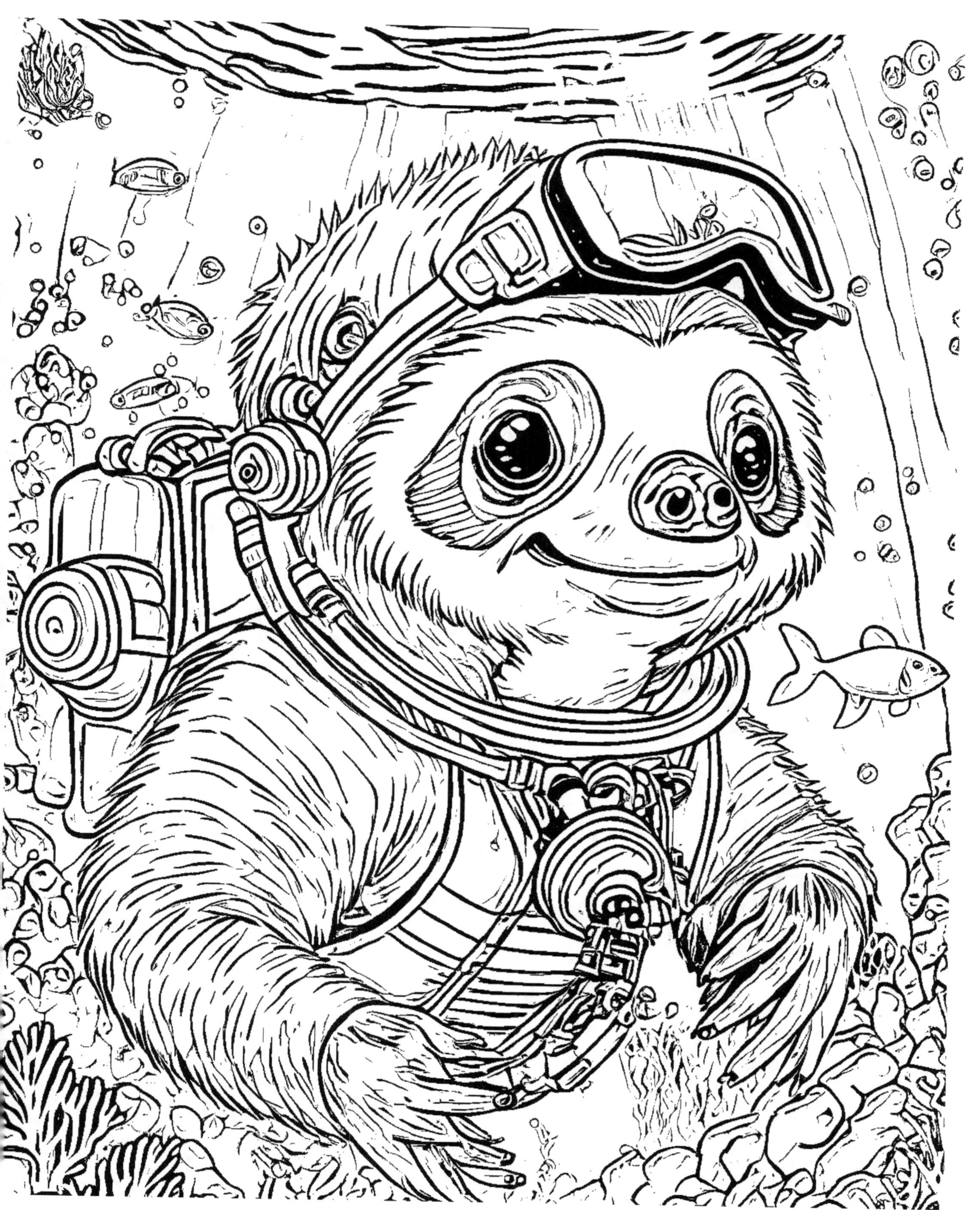

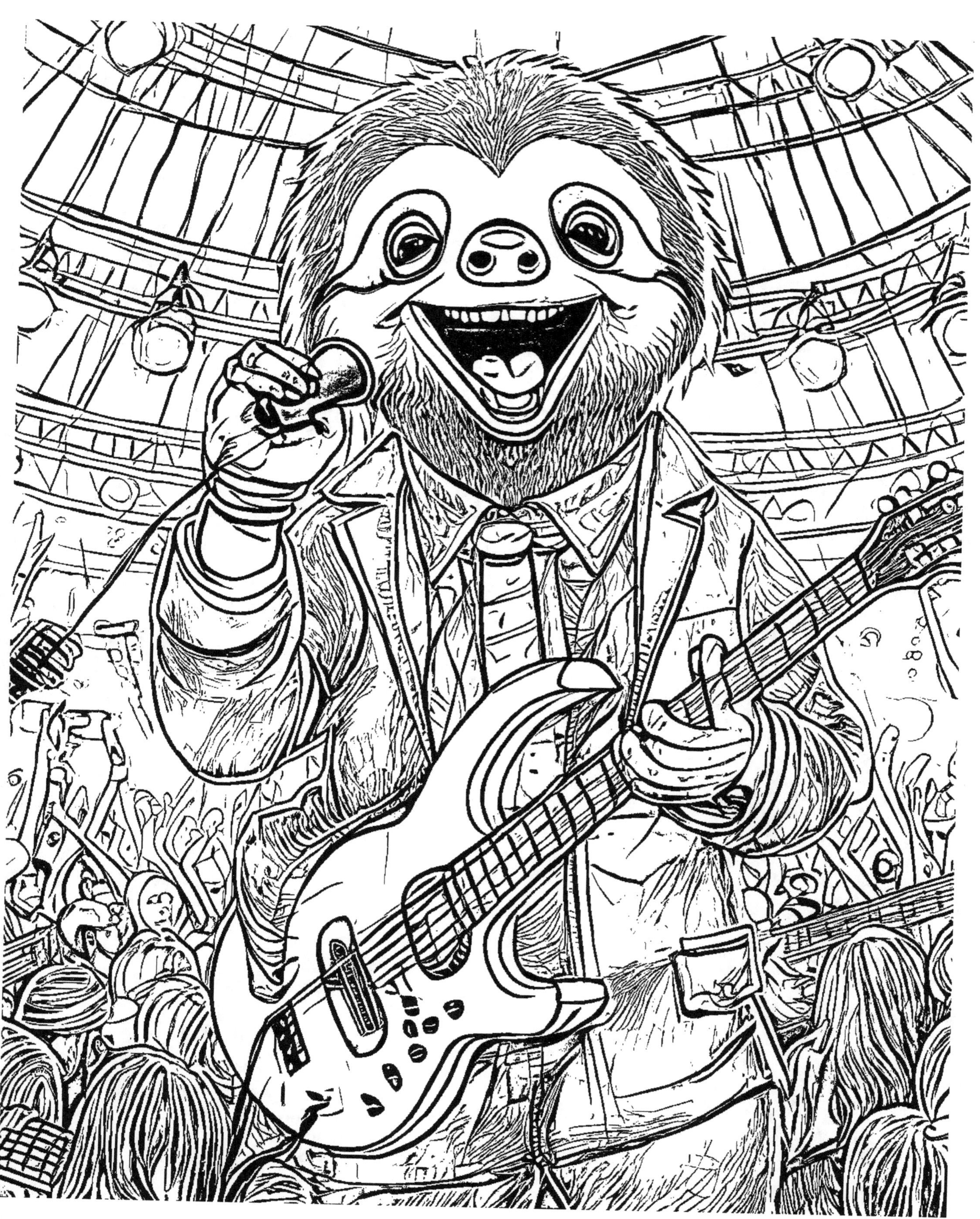

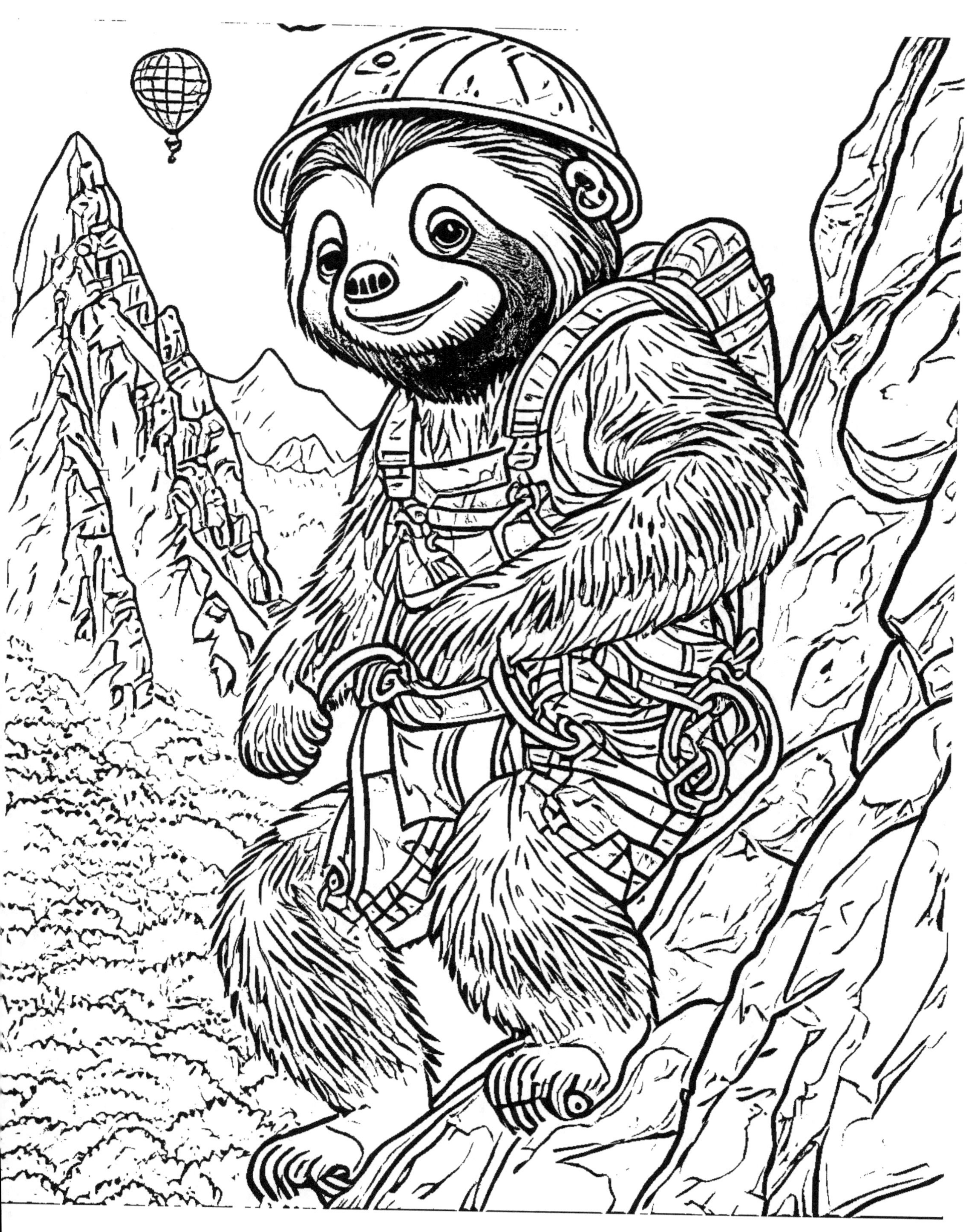

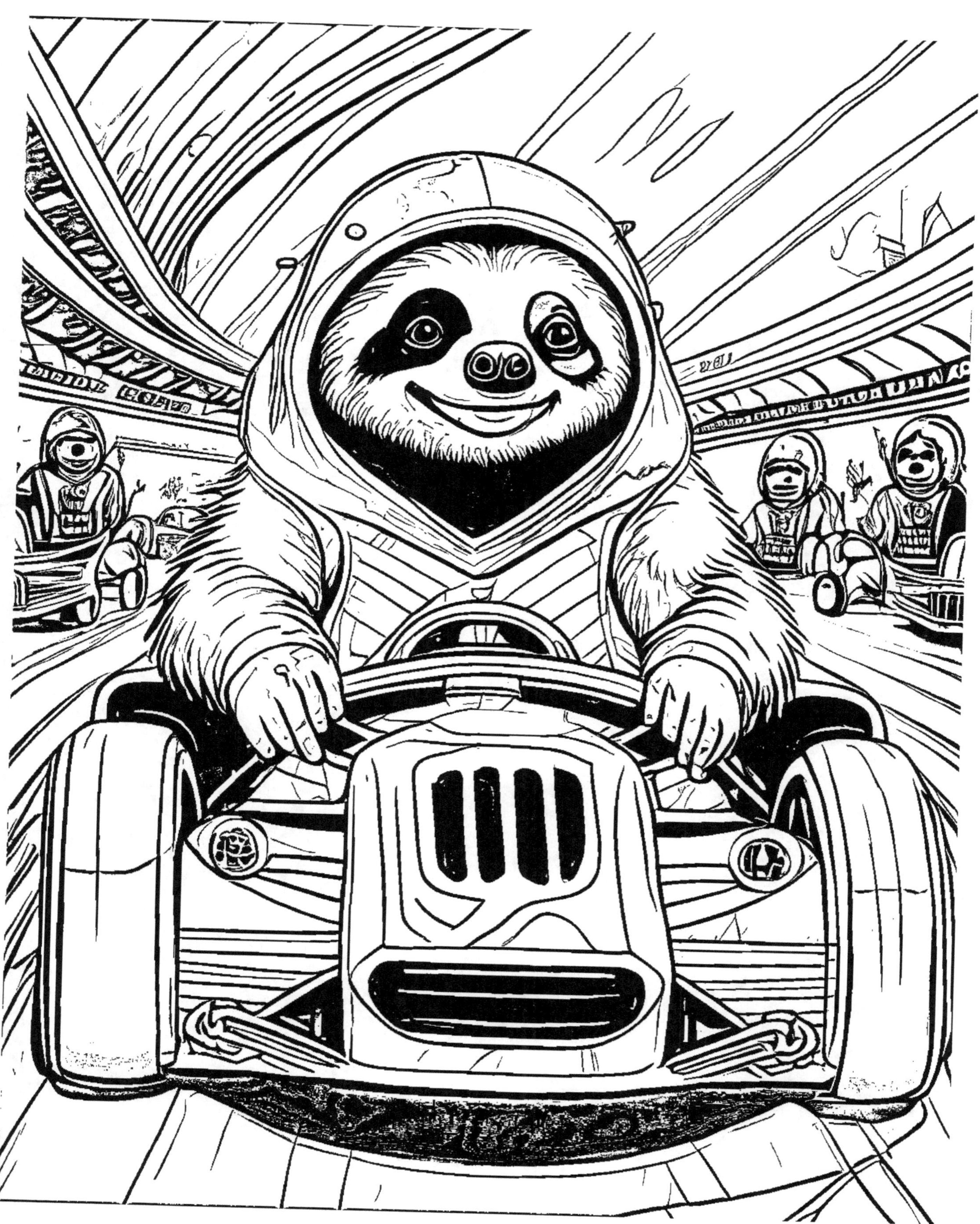

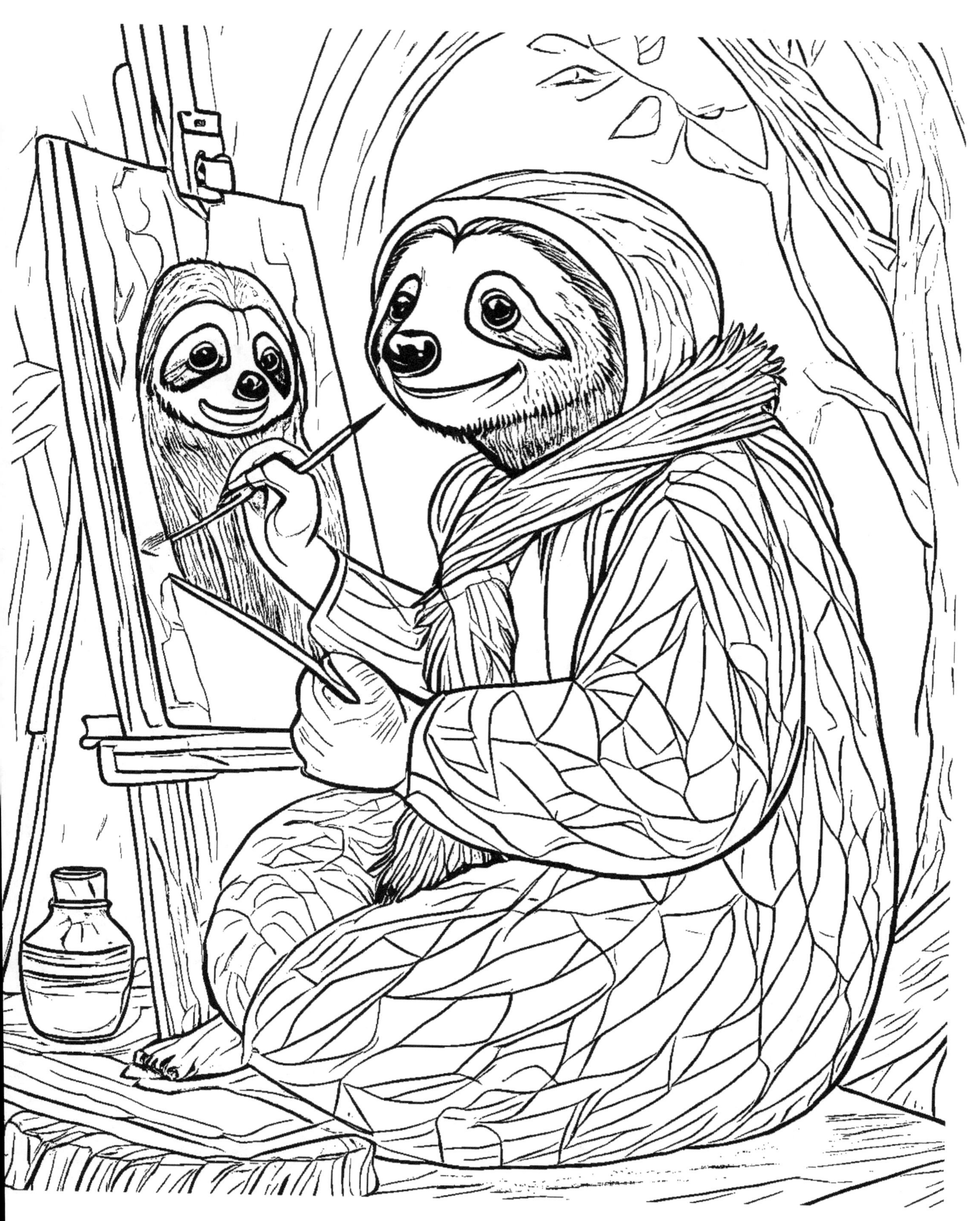

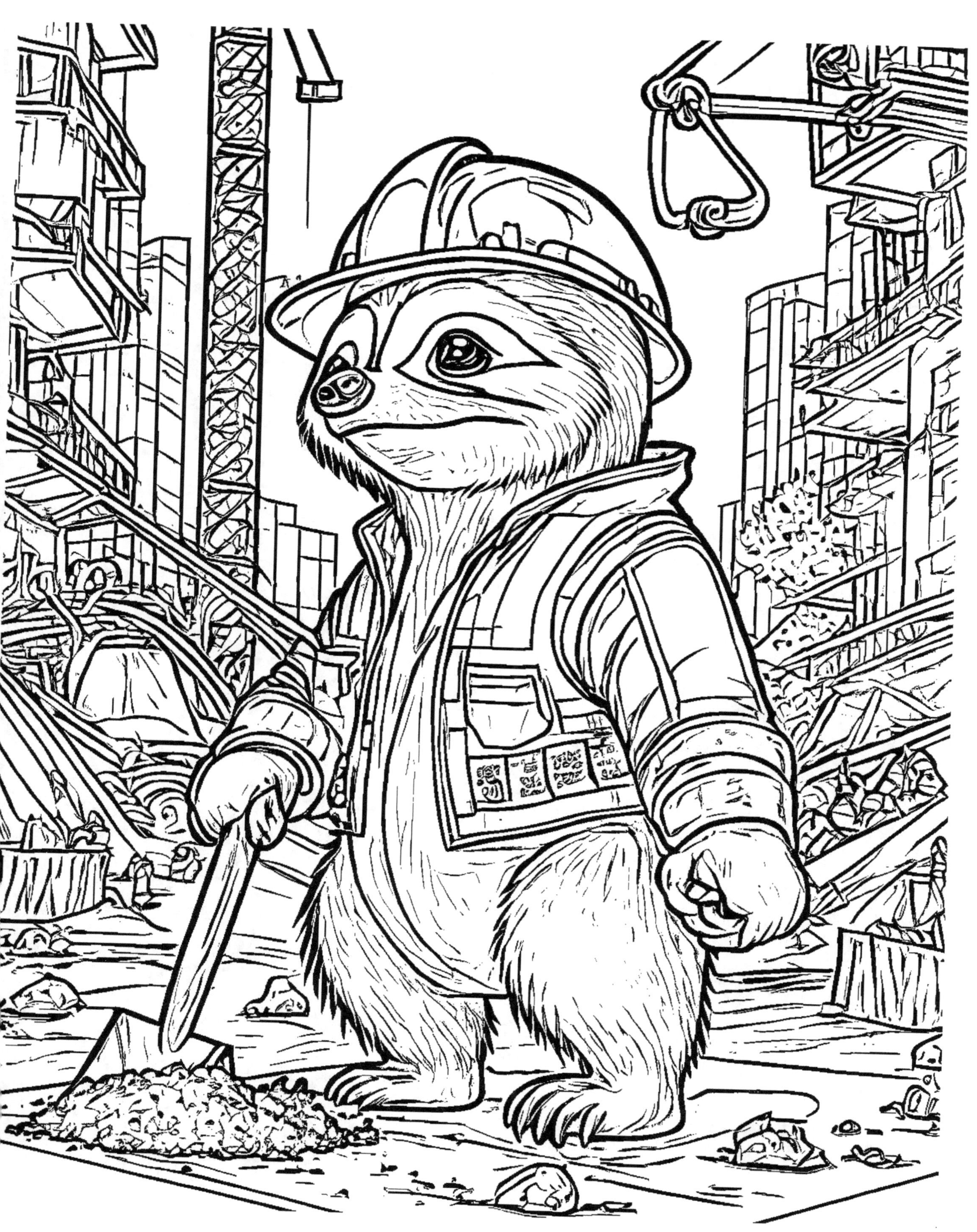

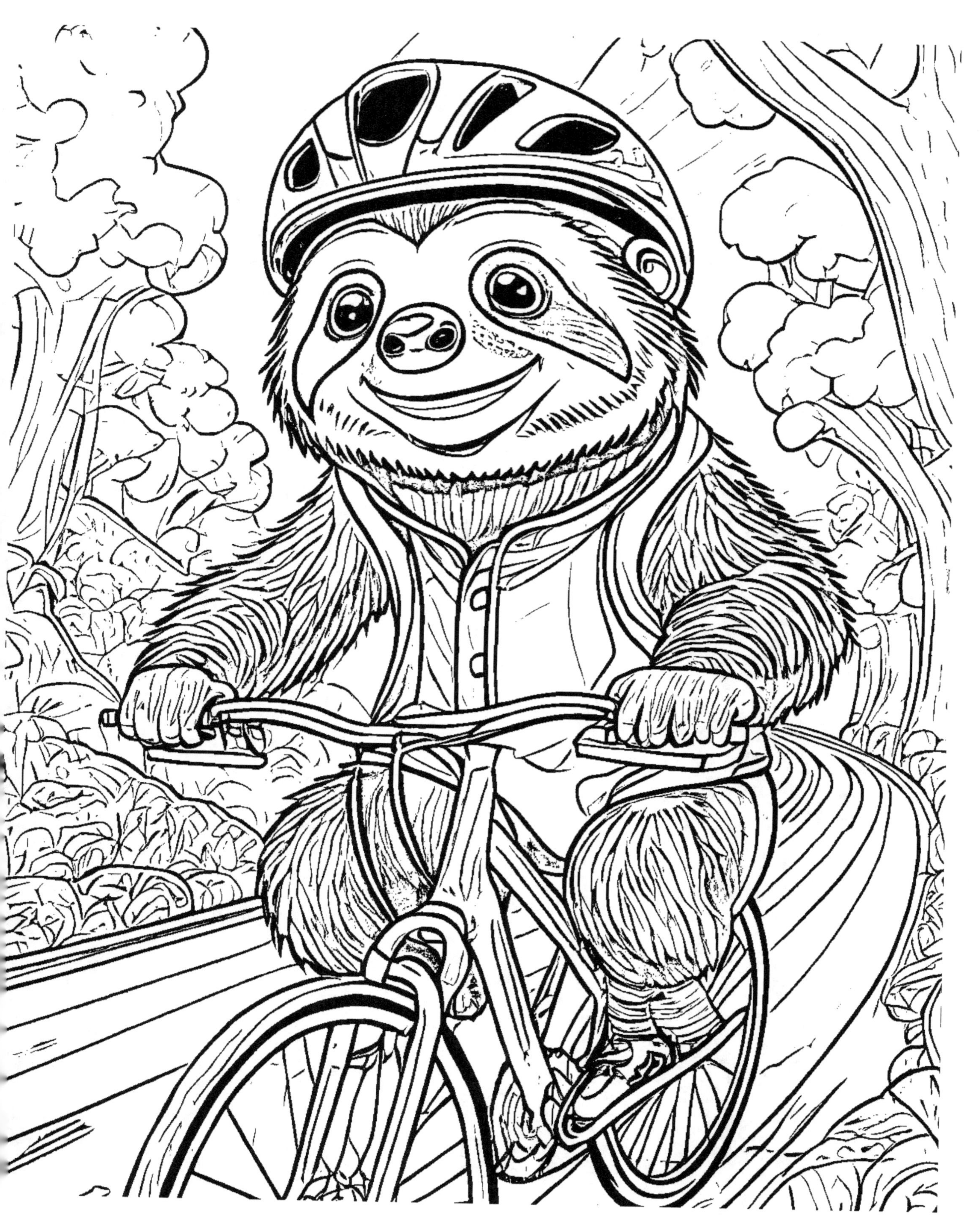

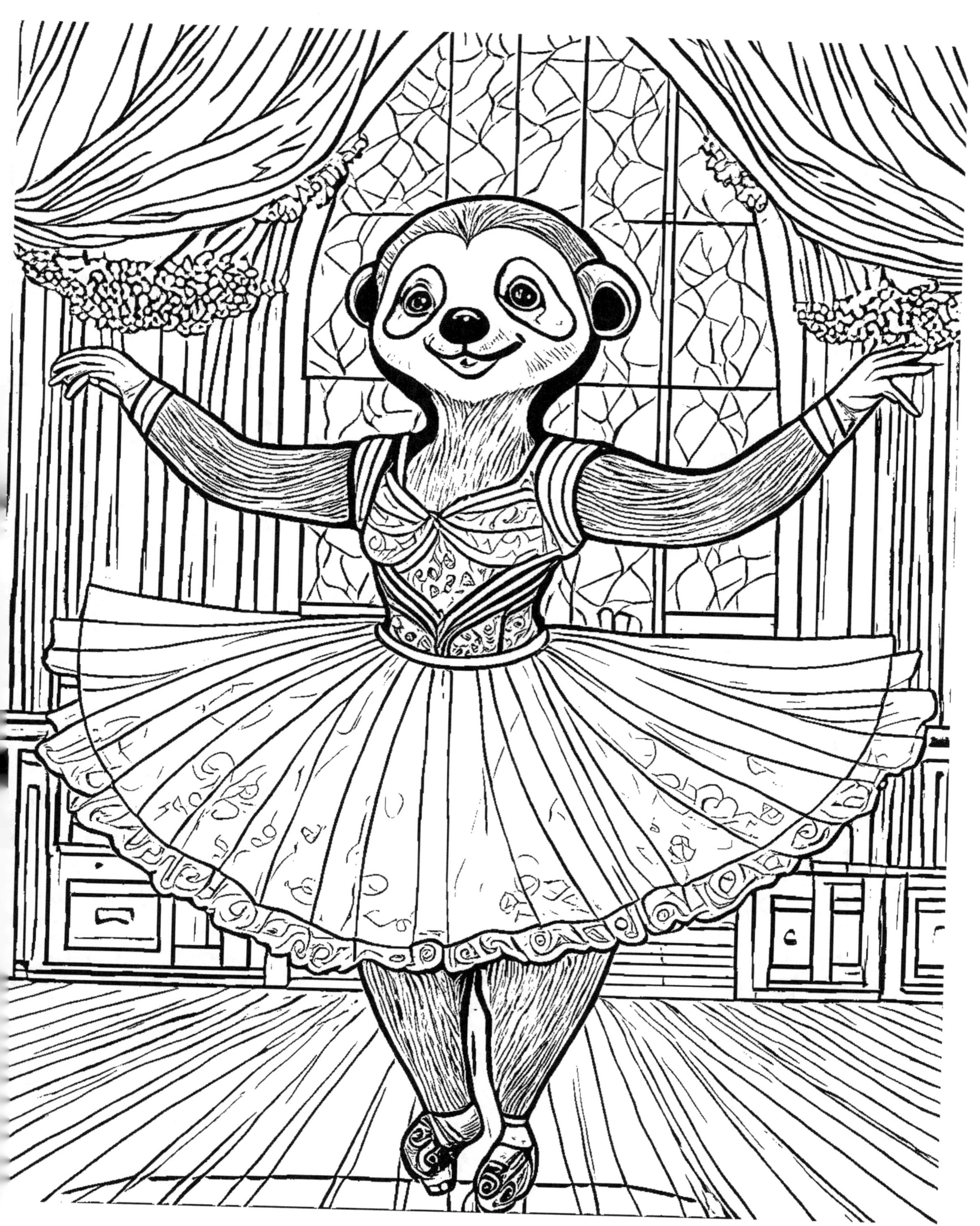

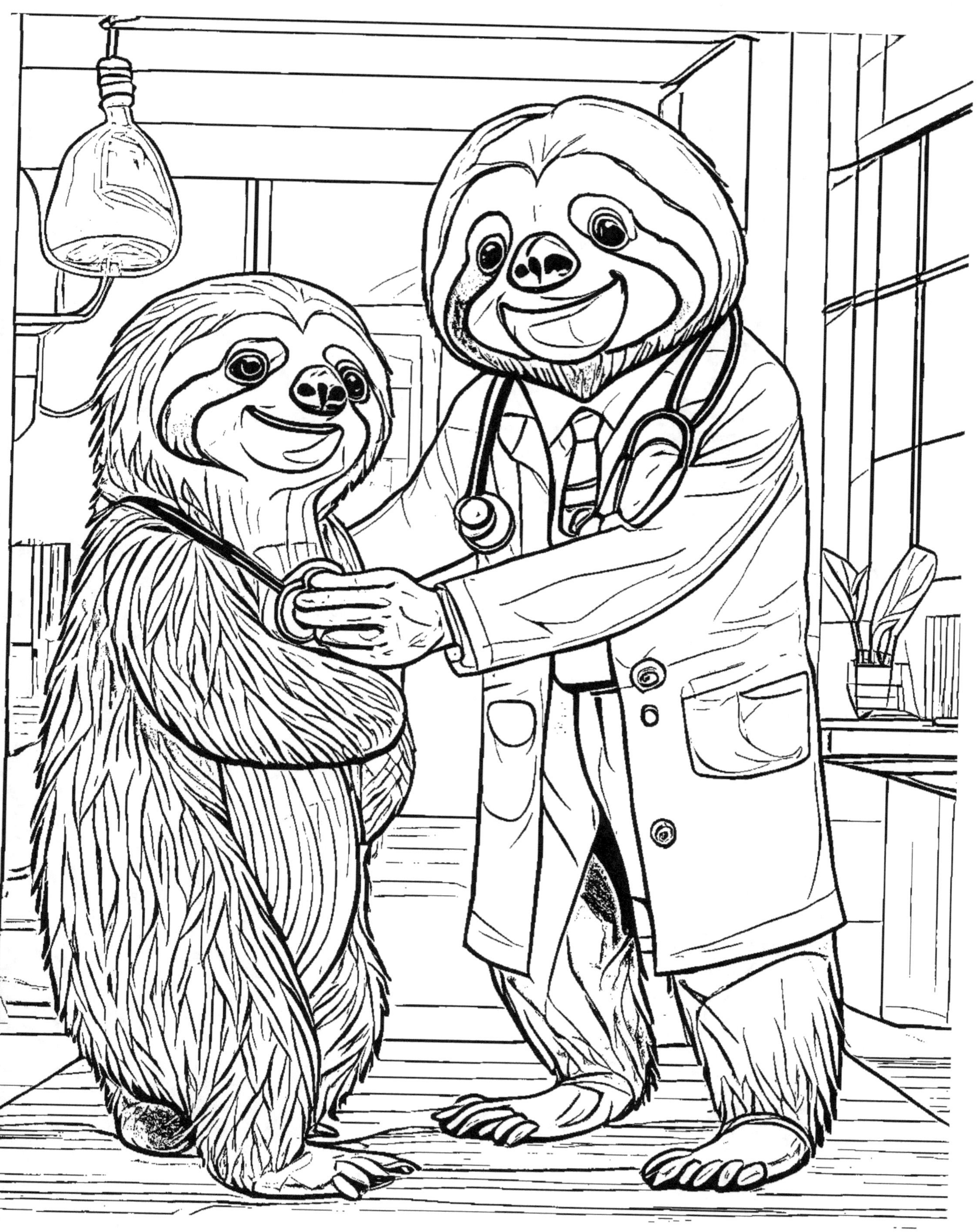

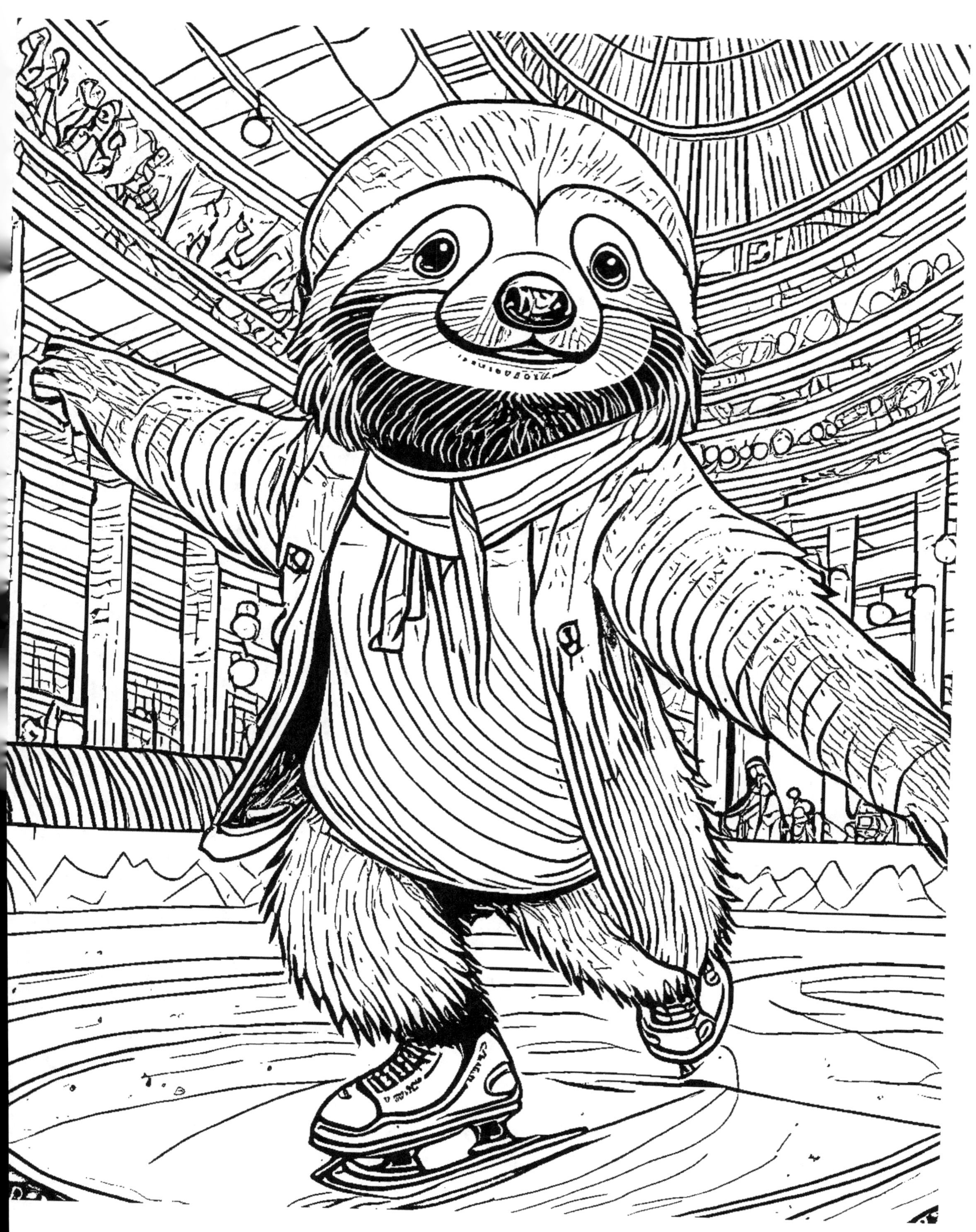

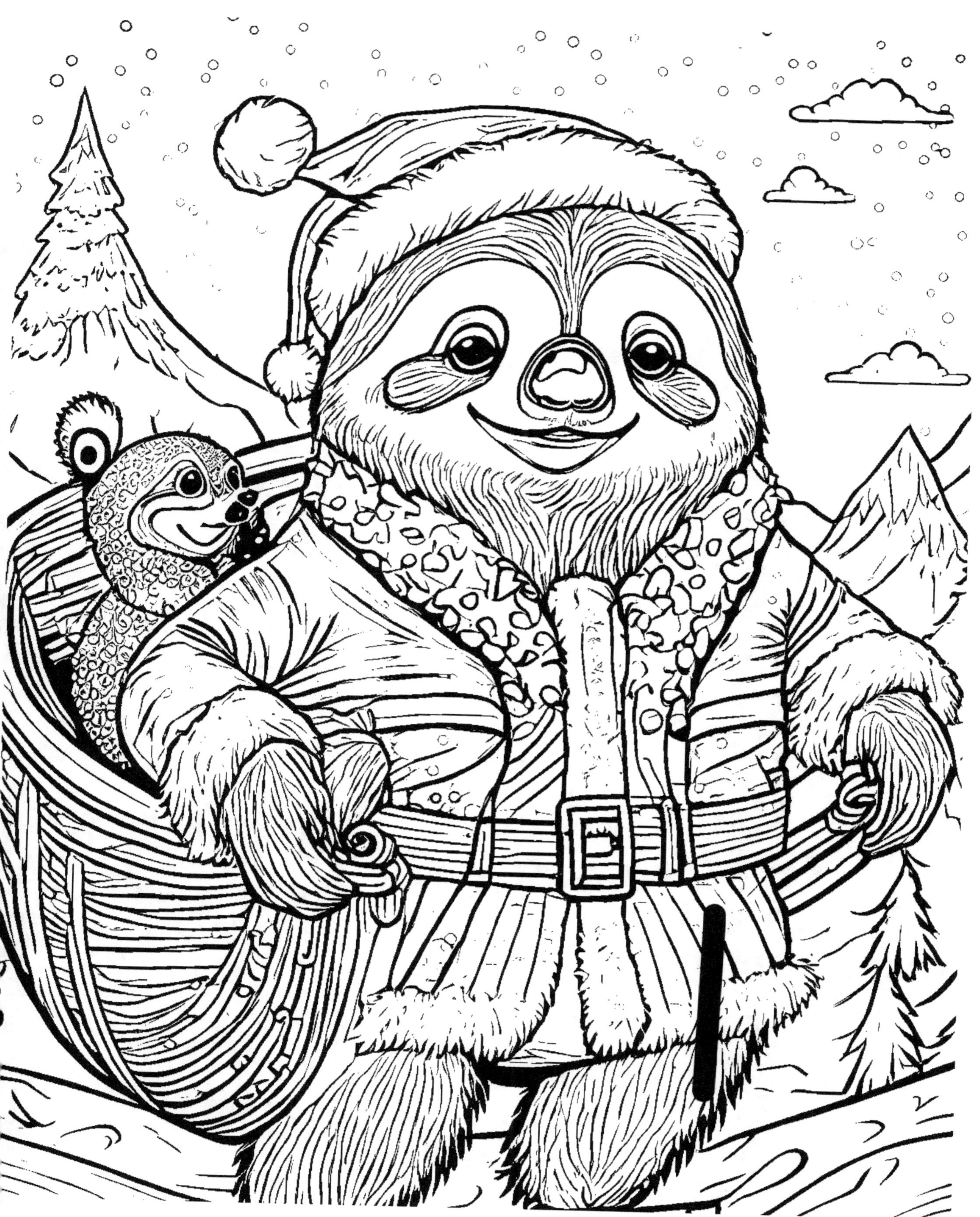

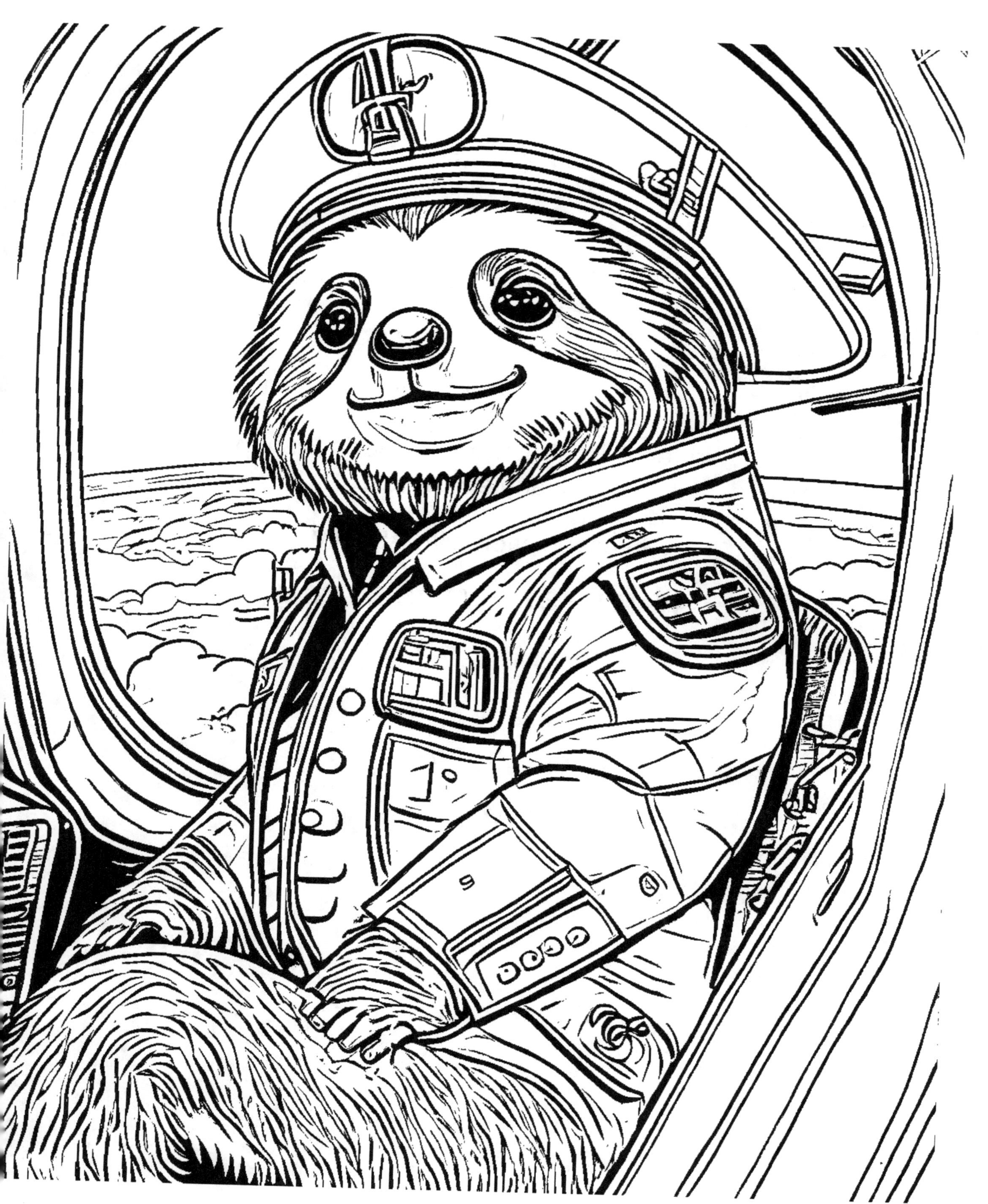

Written & Illustrated by Brandon Bishop
& Jeannie Kotynski

In association with ASY TV

WATCH ASY TV AT ASYTV.COM

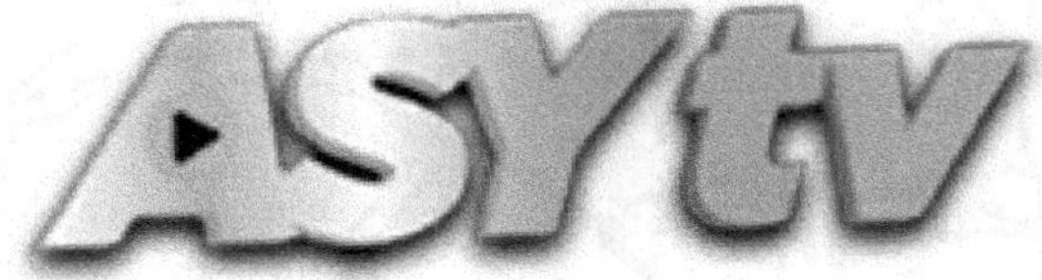

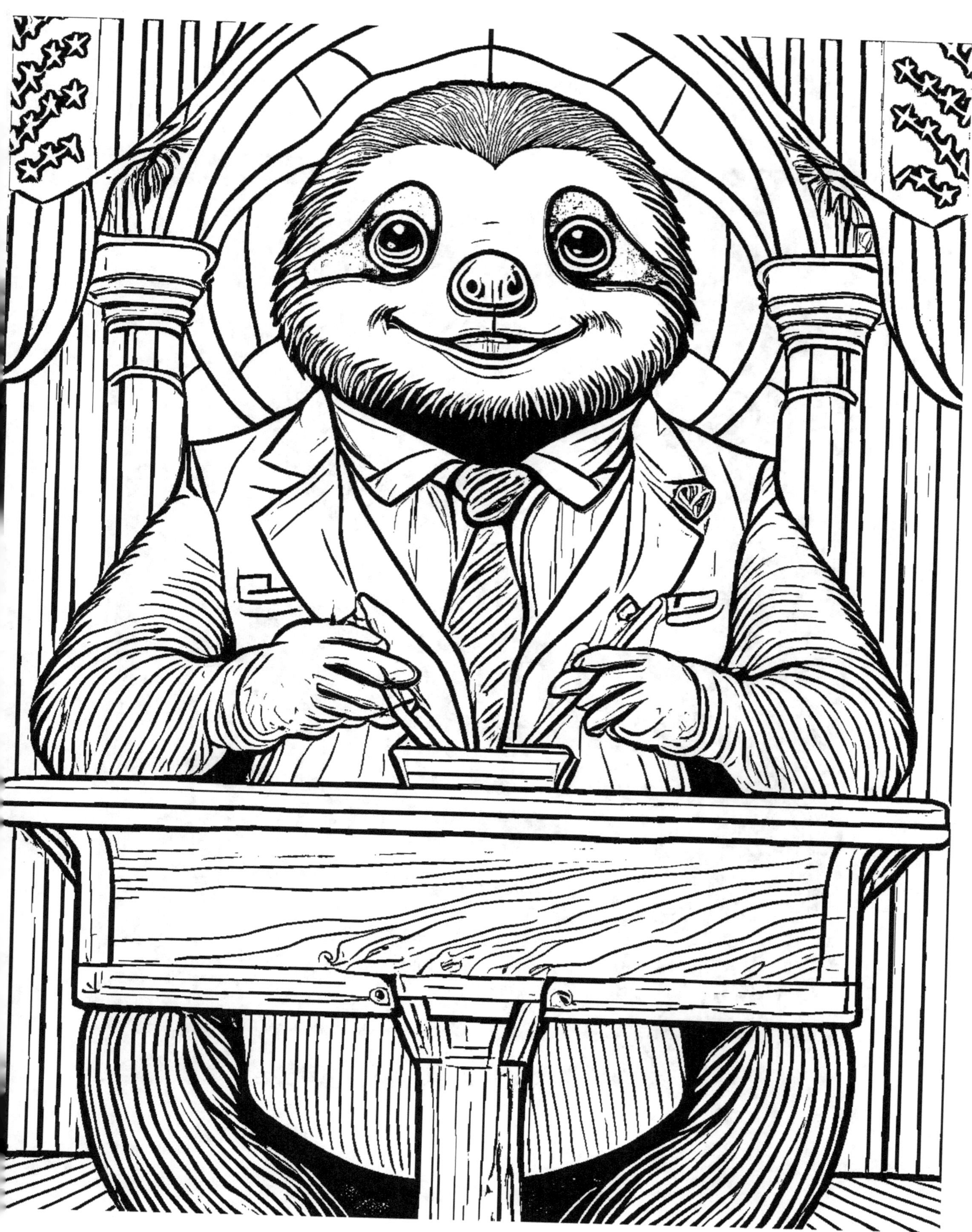

Also available:

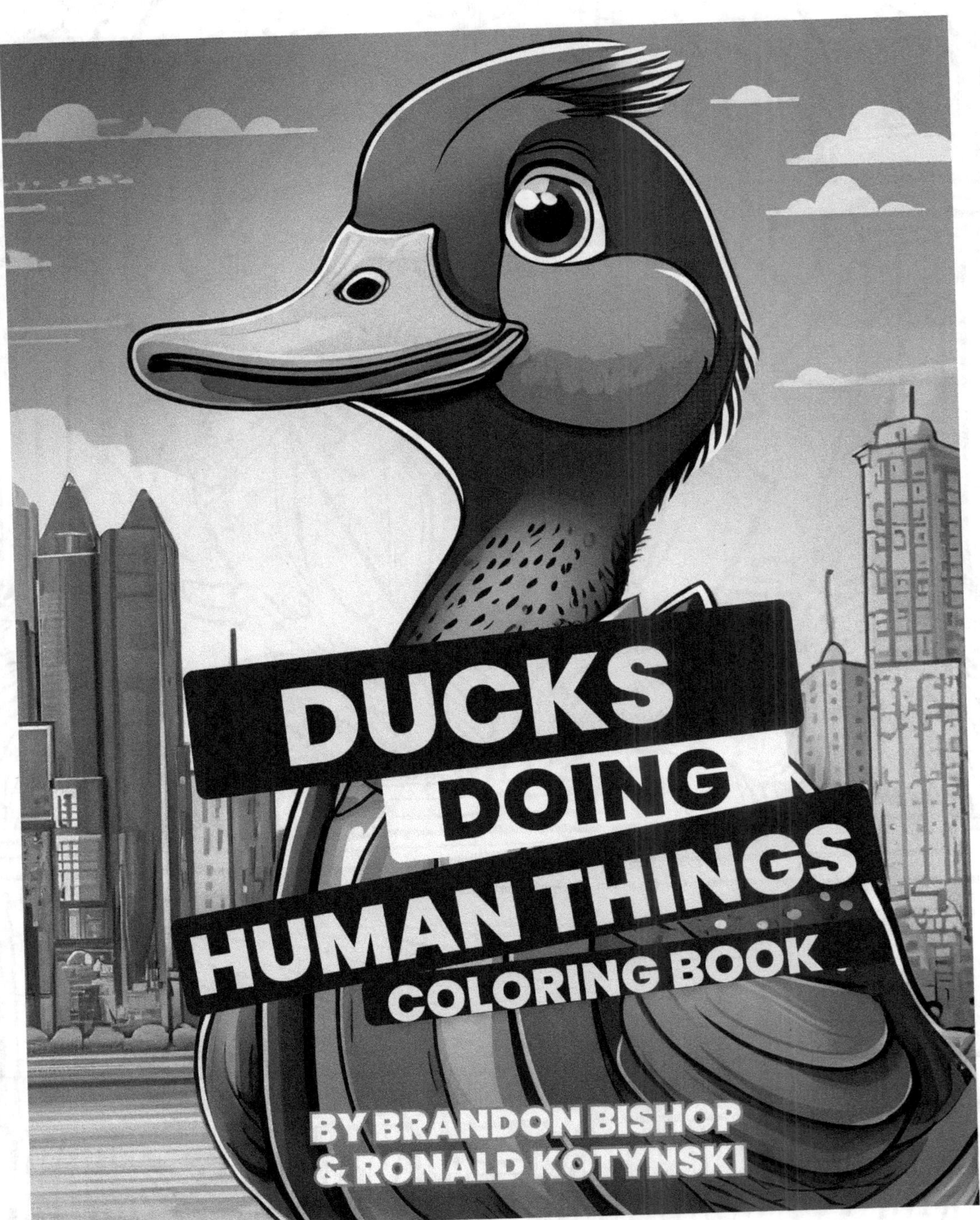

www.ingramcontent.com/pod-product-compliance
Lightning Source LLC
LaVergne TN
LVHW080329110826
845155LV00026B/230